Presented To:

_____

From:

_____

Date:

_____

Introduction

My hope in creating this journal is that girls will experience the benefits of journaling.

Journaling is not just for adults. Young girls deserve to have a safe space to write and express their feelings.

Designed for girls 10 years of age and up, this journal can be used anywhere. There is significant space to write as little or as much as you'd like. There is no required length because the most important thing is to write. You will also find pages for sketching and some positive affirmations to keep you motivated.

After starting on your writing journey, I hope that you are able to see the benefit of journaling and continue to include it into your daily routine.

Happy Journaling!

YOU ARE
BEAUTIFUL

Date:_____

Today, I am feeling....

Date:_____

Today, I am feeling....

Date:_____

Today, I am feeling....

Date:_____

Today, I am feeling....

Date:_____

Today, I am feeling....

Date:_____

Today, I am feeling....

YOU ARE NEEDED

Date:_____

Today, I am feeling....

Date:_____

Today, I am feeling....

Date:_____

Today, I am feeling....

Date:_____

Today, I am feeling....

Date:_____

Today, I am feeling....

Date:_____

Today, I am feeling....

YOU ARE ENOUGH

Date:_____

Today, I am feeling....

Date:_____

Today, I am feeling....

Date:_____

Today, I am feeling....

Date:_____

Today, I am feeling....

_____
_____
_____
_____
_____
_____
_____
_____
_____
_____
_____
_____
_____
_____
_____
_____

Date:_____

Today, I am feeling....

Date:_____

Today, I am feeling....

YOU MATTER

Date:_____

Today, I am feeling....

Date:_____

Today, I am feeling....

Date:_____

Today, I am feeling....

Date:_____

Today, I am feeling....

Date:_____

Today, I am feeling....

Date:_____

Today, I am feeling....

FOLLOW YOUR DREAMS

Date:_____

Today, I am feeling....

Date:_____

Today, I am feeling....

Date:_____

Today, I am feeling....

Date:_____

Today, I am feeling....

_____
_____
_____
_____
_____
_____
_____
_____
_____
_____
_____
_____
_____
_____
_____

Date:_____

Today, I am feeling....

Date:_____

Today, I am feeling....

BELIEVE

Date:_____

Today, I am feeling....

Date:_____

Today, I am feeling....

Date:_____

Today, I am feeling....

Date:_____

Today, I am feeling....

___
___
___
___
___
___
___
___
___
___
___
___
___
___
___

Date:_____

Today, I am feeling....

Date:_____

Today, I am feeling....

DREAM BIG

Date:_____

Today, I am feeling....

Date:_____

Today, I am feeling....

Date:_____

Today, I am feeling....

Date:_____

Today, I am feeling....

Date:_____

Today, I am feeling....

_____
_____
_____
_____
_____
_____
_____
_____
_____
_____
_____
_____
_____
_____
_____

Date:_____

Today, I am feeling....

YOU ARE
SMART

Date:_____

Today, I am feeling....

Date:＿＿＿＿＿＿＿

Today, I am feeling....

Date:_____

Today, I am feeling....

Date:_____

Today, I am feeling....

_____
_____
_____
_____
_____
_____
_____
_____
_____
_____
_____
_____
_____
_____
_____
_____

Date:_____

Today, I am feeling....

Date:_____

Today, I am feeling....

YOU ARE AMAZING

Date:_____

Today, I am feeling....

Date:_____

Today, I am feeling....

Date:_____

Today, I am feeling....

Date:_____

Today, I am feeling....

Date:_____

Today, I am feeling....

Date:_____

Today, I am feeling....

LET YOUR VOICE BE HEARD

Date:_____

Today, I am feeling....

Date:_____

Today, I am feeling....

_____
_____
_____
_____
_____
_____
_____
_____
_____
_____
_____
_____
_____
_____
_____

Date:_____

Today, I am feeling....

_____
_____
_____
_____
_____
_____
_____
_____
_____
_____
_____
_____
_____
_____
_____

Date:_____

Today, I am feeling....

Date:_____

Today, I am feeling....

_____
_____
_____
_____
_____
_____
_____
_____
_____
_____
_____
_____
_____
_____
_____
_____

Date:_____

Today, I am feeling....

_____
_____
_____
_____
_____
_____
_____
_____
_____
_____
_____
_____
_____
_____

ALWAYS DO YOUR BEST

Date:_____

Today, I am feeling....

Date:_____

Today, I am feeling....

_____
_____
_____
_____
_____
_____
_____
_____
_____
_____
_____
_____
_____
_____

Date:_____

Today, I am feeling....

_____
_____
_____
_____
_____
_____
_____
_____
_____
_____
_____
_____
_____
_____
_____

Date:_____

Today, I am feeling....

Date:_____

Today, I am feeling....

Date:_____

Today, I am feeling....

YOU ARE STRONG

Date:_____

Today, I am feeling....

_____
_____
_____
_____
_____
_____
_____
_____
_____
_____
_____
_____
_____
_____
_____

Date:_____

Today, I am feeling....

_____
_____
_____
_____
_____
_____
_____
_____
_____
_____
_____
_____
_____
_____
_____
_____

Date:_____

Today, I am feeling....

Date:_____

Today, I am feeling....

_____
_____
_____
_____
_____
_____
_____
_____
_____
_____
_____
_____
_____
_____
_____

Date:_____

Today, I am feeling....

_____
_____
_____
_____
_____
_____
_____
_____
_____
_____
_____
_____
_____
_____
_____
_____

Date:_____

Today, I am feeling....

Date:_____

Today, I am feeling....

YOU WILL DO GREAT THINGS

www.ingramcontent.com/pod-product-compliance
Lightning Source LLC
Chambersburg PA
CBHW081232080526
44587CB00022B/3921